A FORTUNE TO SHARE

Table of contents

IN CELEBRATION OF VASH YOUNG 3

CHAPTER ONE 5

CHAPTER TWO 15

CHAPTER THREE 21

CHAPTER FOUR 29

CHAPTER FIVE 41

CHAPTER SIX 49

CHAPTER SEVEN 55

CHAPTER EIGHT 63

CHAPTER NINE 69

BLUE RIBBON BOOKS, INC.

NEW YORK CITY

IN CELEBRATION OF VASH YOUNG

SOME years ago, a young man going about his business selling advertising space in one of our best magazines received a vision that changed everything about him except his name. He saw himself and his fellow men in a perspective so different that it gave him new power. He left the work he had and entered a new field where his conception of what he could do for others found remarkable outlet and scope. Here he prospered amazingly. His own account of the ways in which his new philosophy worked has a fascination which few stories of human success can equal.

There is nothing so practical as idealism. Vash Young has lived his ideal, and what is more, has written this moving account of his career, giving chapter and verse for each successive experience, to show how he did it.

Here is the cure for our economic ills. There has never been a time in our industrial history when right thinking was so badly needed. This little book should find its way into the hands and minds of the whole army of unemployed and unsatisfied. The only way to reorganize the world is for each of us to reorganize himself. is what Vash Young did, and immediately he found himself living and working in a very different world.

If people find out what is in this book; its sales will be enormous. Every company employing salesmen should put a copy in the hands of each. Particularly insurance companies. It should be a text-book in all schools of business— all schools of every character, for that matter. It describes the only method of salesmanship that is without a flaw, that has no drawback. Its principles are as applicable to advertising as to sales Manship. The first big advertiser who puts into his advertising such a conception toward competition and humility toward his own business will sweep the markets of the country like a prairie fire. Strictly it is not a business book, but in any list of business books it stands, I think, at the topo

EARNEST ELMO CALKINS

CHAPTER ONE
A FORTUNE TO SHARE

I AM one of those lucky fellows who inherited a great fortune.

It came to me after years of poverty and reckless living, and as the result of the death of a man whose passing I had no cause to regret.

Under such conditions of inheritance it is no more than just that I should share the fortune with others. There is enough of it to go around no matter how many of you take your cut, for it is not the kind of wealth that is affected by bank failures, stock-market crashes, or business depressions. It has survived such happenings, it has been divided many times, and to-day it is larger than ever before. In a manner seemingly strange, division has the effect of multiplication upon this wealth of mine.

The man who bequeathed riches to me resembled me in every outward way. His name was the same as mine. He had the same parents, the same childhood, the same early manhood. As a matter of fact, he was my former self. Yes, after a long and suffering illness my former self gave up a fruitless struggle and died. The autopsy showed he died of selfishness, pessimism, fear, worry, indecision, vain regrets, stewing about business, irritability, envy, false desires and other complications.

But this old Vash Young wasn't wholly bad, for he left to me a great store of optimism, courage, contentment, dominion over business worries, patience, and freedom from harmful appetites.

I took this inheritance out into the business world, and it has made me successful beyond my fondest hopes. I started giving it away, and soon discovered that the more I gave the more I had. Men and women of great affairs began coming to me bringing business with them. It often happens that the man who pursues the dollar too diligently finds it hard to catch, but if he will pursue some other and better goal, dollars come around to see what sort of fellow he is.

This old Vash Young was an advertising salesman, who was doing nothing worth speaking of. When he died, his job was gone, and his beneficiary found himself an insurance salesman, starting from scratch in the most highly competitive of occupations. It looked like seven lean years ahead. An acquaintance of mine, learning that I had cut loose from regular pay checks and started out on a precarious commission basis with less than a hundred dollars, and with a wife and daughter to care for, was decidedly alarmed.

"Vash, you are in a hell of a fix!" said he, Outwardly, I was. But inwardly I was in a heaven of a fix, for I had challenged negative thinking to a death battle and had won the pre liminary skirmish. There is no finer sensation in life than that which comes with victory over one's self. It feels good to go fronting into a hard wind, winning against its power, but it feels a thousand times better to go forward to a goal of inward achievement, brushing aside all your old internal enemies as you advance.

I know the joy of skating on a clear cold day. I know the joy of getting of a perfect drive in golf. I know the delight of a fine meal after a long walk These are real and wholesome, but all of them put together cannot approach the thrill of ridding yourself of fear!

" Prosperity cannot be built on fear!" How often have you seen that statement since the collapse of inflated values and inflated ideas jolted us in the autumn of 1929? Hundreds of times, probably, and it was true every time you saw it. If men are afraid, they cannot work effectively, and they will not spend anything more than is absolutely necessary. I know what I am talking about, for I have tried both fear and courage, and fear produced nothing but unhappiness, while courage produced a good living and a whole lot of fun.

That morning after I had buried my former self, and found my new self-jobless, with enough money to last but two or three weeks, and with a brave wife and daughter trusting me to care for them, I sat down and did some thinking.

Two courses were open to me. One was to get panicky, to say the fortune that had been left me was intangible, academic, of no practical value. This was a fine chance to indulge in some self-pity. The other course was to claim my fortune, give it a try and find out whether or not it was negotiable. I chose the latter course and have found that fortune negotiable in coin of the realm, and in happiness. The result is that I am a confirmed optimist, the most gullible man in the world, believing all the good things said about life.

But to get to this point I had to stop thinking about myself, to forget the past, to leave the future to care for itself and to concentrate on to-day. I calmly realized that we had always had a place to sleep, something to eat and something to wear. As these three essentials were all we actually needed and as we had always had them, why worry that someday we would not have them?

Doubts tried to creep into my mind, but every time a negative thought came to me, I stopped, mentally if not physically, challenged it, thrust it out of my consciousness and thought of something worth-while. This is a habit any one can acquire. Try it some time. At first the unwholesome thoughts of fear, impatience and the like will struggle, but they are not strong enough to win if you give them the whole works. Crowd them out of your mind. Think of something pleasant You as well, for thinking of unpleasant things will do no good. If you are going to starve anyway, you might as well do it with as little preliminary suffering as possible. There have many occasions I found it helpful to talk out loud to my own thoughts, ordering the unwholesome ones to go off somewhere and jump into the river. If anyone had listened to one of these conversations he probably would have thought me crazy, but it does not matter to me what any one might think. The important thing for me is to get rid of an unwholesome, weakening thought or emotion.

This victory over my own mental processes, I think I have won. It has been a long time now since I have had a real battle to fight with doubt, fear or envy, or any of the other mental parasites that afflict life so cruelly. Some time ago I had been working on a prospect for a large insurance policy. He was about ready to take a quarter of a million dollars, and that would have meant a whole lot to me. He did take that policy, but from another agent, and one day when I happened to see him at lunch, he told me, stammering and full of embarrassment, what he had done.

There was just a fleeting second of disappointment for me. Resentment, envy of the successful agent tried to rise up, but only for a flash. Almost immediately I was delighted that the man had taken out such a large policy, and I told him so. It will be a fine thing for him and his family to have this security, this protection against poverty. And it certainly was a fine thing for the agent who landed the insurance. I went back to my office walking on air, for this was final proof to me that I had gained over disappointment. Immediately, to put myself and my emotion on record, I wrote a letter to my rival agent telling him how glad I was he had been so successful. And I meant it. No kidding, I really meant it. Proof that I had won a fight meant more to me than any commission. I am not in business, anyhow, to make money, but to live as happy a life as my potentialities will permit.

None the less, perhaps partly because of my attitude, I get my share of business. For some years I have been among the hundred leading agents in America. The largest insurance policy ever written by an agent without assistance was written by me, and without solicitation on my part. Here is how it happened.

One day a friend told me his wife's mother had died and he could do nothing to console his wife. He asked me if I would mind going home with him to talk to her. Of course, I did not mind. A condition of the will left by my former self required that I put any distress call ahead of any business call, and I had accepted the obligation of that will, along with its benefits. When we reached the stricken home, we found me friend's wife deep in grief. After a bit of common-sense reasoning, she saw that it was her duty to be brave. Once she got hold of positive ideas, she braced up immediately, and from that moment forth she seemed like a different person.

A few days later I had a call to see a man whom I had never met. He turned out to be a brother of the woman whom I had visited, and when I had taken a seat in his office, he began at once to thank me for what I had done.

"Do you get paid for doing things like that?" he asked.

"Not in gold," I said, "but in other ways that mean more to me."

"Well, it's gold I'm talking about," he declared.

He then asked me to present him a plan for insurance for his young son, and I submitted an illustration based upon a twenty-five-thousand-dollar policy. He studied the figures and then said:

"Make it two hundred and fifty thousand."

The next morning the son was examined for the insurance and found to be a first-class risk, but the father was not yet satisfied. Before the policy had gone through, he asked me what the largest amount of insurance was ever placed on a boy. A little study showed that Jackie Coogan had four hundred and fifty thousand dollars in force at that time.

"Then get me half a million!" demanded my new friend.

Another few days passed, and the face of the policy was lifted again, this time to three-quarters of a million, and even that was not the end, for the final count was a policy for one million and sixty-five thousand dollars on that boy! This came to me without one bit of solicitation, and from a stranger. Just a break, some salesmen have said, and a whale of a break at that. But it does not stand alone in my experience, though it is the largest policy I have written. This was only one of the times when my fortune proved negotiable in coin of the realm.

Since I changed my view-point of life, things have been happening swiftly. I was utterly unknown at the time I came into my fortune. Before long, however, I was making some headway in my new line. Then some of my clients gave me a testimonial dinner at one of the big New York hotels. Next my story was told in newspapers and magazines, and after that I was called on frequently to make public addresses. I have spoken from coast to coast, always at the invitation of some business group. These talks seem to me to be well' received, for literally thousands of requests have come to me for copies of them, and one magazine article I wrote has been in such demand that more than twenty-five thousand copies of it were distributed after the magazine could no longer be bought.

Such recognition as this astonishes me, for I am not a college man, not even a high-school graduate. In fact, I never finished grammar school. Just an ordinary human being, an average sort of fellow who stumbled into a fortune which is available to anyone and everyone in the world. I think it is the complete simplicity, the obvious common sense of my program of life that has made it seem worth-while to so many persons. Suppose you are up against it; does it do any good to make bad matters worse by crippling your mental capacities with worry and fear? No man can add one dollar to his bank account by worrying. If he could, there would be countless millionaires in this country right now as a result of the business collapse of 1929.

Just what did happen in 1929? To me the answer is very plain. It is simply this: the getting habit was rudely interrupted. This is not a new experience for that habit. It has been interrupted from time to time ever since the world began, and there never will be a time when it will be free from interruptions, because you simply cannot stabilize self-interest. Back in 1928 many of our leaders were saying that every man in America could get enough money to make him secure. Poverty, they said, would be abolished by getting. But poverty certainly has not been abolished. All of us now see how sorely wrong those optimistic predictions were, and they were wrong not because there is an upward limit to prosperity, but because we were going at life from the wrong approach. Self-interest expanded too much. Greed for easy money grew to alarming proportions. Young men out of college felt no need to go to work but sat around in brokers' offices "getting rich." Nobody thought about giving. Getting and spending—that was the order of the day.

The result was inevitable. When people are not satisfied with a fair return, when they seek millions without effort, but one thing can happen, and that thing did happen. Within a few weeks paper values crumbled, and paper millinarias woke up with terrible headaches. " We are ruined!" they wailed. Not at all, unless they chose to continue to think so.

The transition from silly optimism to bumps of reality wasn't easy, and for a year many leaders continued to say that everything was all fight. Business was always turning the comer, and seemingly it got very dizzy from too many turns, for it certainly tottered. Frantic appeals were addressed to the public. " Buy now and bring back prosperity!" begged business men. They should have added two words, making the appeal read: "Buy now and bring back prosperity to me!" Then, at least, the appeal would have had the advantage of being honest. The old getting habit dies hard.

Suppose at the very beginning of the panic, business had sent out the appeal which it did begin to send out, two years later? Suppose it had turned swiftly and sought at once to give the public the greatest possible values, might not the time of depression have been shortened. Here is what business should have said:

"There is nothing to be alarmed about. We are one hundred and twenty million strong in a rich and fertile land. We have half the gold in the world, half the machinery and the will to overcome obstacles. We appreciate your confidence and support and during this re-adjournment period we are taking steps to give you the biggest run for your money you ever have received. We are going to give you better merchandise, better service and better prices. We know that you have problems to meet, and we wish to help you solve them. Sincerely yours, United States Business."

That appeal, in substance, did go out two years after the blow-up, and it will mark the real beginning of the up-turn in prosperity, for it marks the return of the giving habit. I do not know economic laws very well, but I have always noticed that the man who gives the most for the money, gets the most business. The giving habit is a lot safer than the habit. It is sounder business. But maybe I'm going out over my depth now, so I'll come back to individual cases.

Unemployment! What a ghastly word that has become. The mere thought of millions of men walking the streets in quest of work is horrible. Scores of these men have come to me. Probably hundreds of them, for I give each Saturday to people who are in trouble. On my office schedule. it is known as "Trouble Day." My greatest hope in talking with worried souls is to give them a new look at life. If they can change their thinking, they certainly will be happier, even if no richer in money, and very often it is true that a man with an affirmative philosophy lands the job. Let me tell you a story.

About nine-thirty last Christmas Eve as I was returning home, a young man stopped me on the street and asked me if I would help him ger something to eat. "Surely, son, I will help you get something to eat, but you are pretty young to be doing this sort of thing. You have a long way to go yet, and this certainly is not the way to start."

I gave him some money and went on my way. The next morning, which was Christmas Day, a very unusual thing occurred. I left my home early to call on my brother, who has two fine boys, and I wanted to see them with their Christmas things. On the way I stopped for a bit of breakfast in a side-arm lunch-room. As I sat down in one of the chairs, I was greatly surprised to see my young friend of the night before sitting opposite me. He had got a shave in the course of the night, which increased my interest in him. I greeted him cordially and asked if he would have something to eat. He replied that he was too discouraged to eat.

" I guess we will have to prove to you that your Heavenly Father is looking out for you," I said. " Here is some money to get through the

day, and here's my address. If you will come to my house at eight o'clock to-night, I shall be glad to have a little talk with you."

Promptly at eight he showed up. We had some guests and were just finishing our meal, but Mrs. Young sat him right down at the dining-room table and gave him a good Christmas dinner. After he had finished I took him into my study and got his story. He had been out of work for several months and had got so shabby that it was impossible for him even to see anybody, much less get a job.

"You haven't been unemployed all these months," I said to him, "you have been working overtime. You have been toiling and slaving, but for the wrong boss. You have been working for failure, discouragement, fear and worry, and the sad part of it is that there has been no salary for your labors. You seem to be destitute, but I am going to tell you how to become rich overnight. I want you to deposit the following thoughts in your mental bank to-night: "I am not afraid.—I am a success, not a failure.—I have an inexhaustible supply of courage, energy, confidence and perseverance."

His face brightened, and I knew that he had caught the idea.

Then with Mrs. Young's help, we got together a suit of clothes, some shoes, socks, underwear, shirts, ties, collars, handkerchiefs, and gave them to him. We also paid his room rent for a week and gave him some money to buy food for a few days. As he was leaving my home, I said:

"Remember to draw upon your new bank account when you need it."

About a week later this young fellow called upon me one evening and I could scarcely recognize him. He was all dressed up and cleaned up, and excitedly told me that he had a job.

"I was coming over from Brooklyn the other morning on the subway," he related, "and I heard one man say to another, ' Mr. So-and-So is looking for a man to do office work.' I immediately remembered what you told me about my bank-account, so I drew out a large hunk of courage and said to this man, 'Would you mind giving me the name and address of your friend who is looking for someone to do office work? I can do that kind of work and need a job very badly.' After a little questioning, the man gave me the name of his friend and I went down and got the job!"

You may call that what you wish, but to me self-confidence and affirmative thinking wrought the change in the young man.

CHAPTER TWO

MY JUNK FACTORY

MOST men look back on their childhood with a surge of sentiment. "Those were the happy days!" they say. A friend of mine, who has interviewed hundreds of men for newspapers and magazines, told me the best way to get a man to talk freely is to remind him of some boyhood experience, or boyhood scene. Lead him to tell of his early experiences and he will become equally talkative about his adventures in mature life. No doubt that is true in most cases, and I wish it were true in mine. But it is not, for my own childhood was far from romantic. I was born in Salt Lake City where my people had lived since my great-grandfather, a brother of Brigham Young, had come there to settle. My mother died when I was fourteen, and her death was a cruel blow to me. For years and years, I grieved for her. My dad, fine man that he is, never fitted into the neighborhood, but went off to Alaska when the gold-rush was on, and we who remained home awaited eagerly the barrel of gold we were confident he would bring back with him. He came back, but his pockets, like those of most prospectors, were empty.

I lived with my grandmother, went to school for a few years, came to regard poverty as the natural condition of life and had no plans or ambitions whatever for myself. There were five of us children, and our grandparents shared gladly with us the meager living they earned. Sometimes we had beans, almost nothing but beans, day after day, but grandfather none the less offered thanks to God before each meal. That is, he offered thanks until the beans appeared once too often. This time he merely lit into the food, with no preliminaries at all. "Why, Pa! Aren't you going to ask a blessing to-night?" asked my grandmother, "No!" said the old gentleman. I'll give no thanks, for I'll be damned if I'm grateful for these beans!"

My sister and I used to team together and do a lot of housework. Making beds, washing dishes, beating and sweeping rugs and carpets and helping with the washing on wash-days were our chores. Wash-day was always on Monday, and I used to hurry home from school to pitch in and help. One fine day, however, there was a football game on, and I wanted to see it. Very quietly I sneaked up to the front porch, grabbed my dilapidated old bicycle and struck out for the game. My sister called to me as I wheeled around the corner, but I pretended not to hear her, although I can see her to this day standing by the tub in our back yard and shrieking to me to come and help with the clothes. I watched that football game with a heavy heart and suffered many pangs of remorse when I thought of my grandmother and my sister washing the clothes by themselves, and I was punished physically as well as mentally for my neglect of duty. Starting home, I hopped on my bicycle at the top of a steep hill in order to make haste. It was not long before I was going so fast my feet left the pedals and in a wild attempt to dodge persons and vehicles I steered for a ditch into which I went head first. I was badly bruised, and the bicycle smashed. My elders said the punishment was meted out to me as a lesson. I do not know whether it was meted out or not, but I do know it was a lesson. I never again ran away from a wash-day.

That incident in itself is not important, except that it illustrates the kind of childhood I had, and the almost invariable ending to my adventures. Time and time again, as a boy, I was humiliated. I celebrated my first day in long pants by going to a dance where I fell sprawling on the floor, and was so ashamed that I jumped up, ran away and left my girl to get home the best way she could. Again, as I was passing my girl's house, the horse I was riding shied, and I fell, together with a sack of sugar, on to the road. The sugar spilled all over the place. I ran and hid in shame. My first job, which I had to take when not more than fifteen, was assistant to a fruit peddler. It seemed all right to me until a little girl told me snootily, "We never deal with peddlers!" Thereupon I resigned, ashamed of what I was doing. My effort as assistant to a tailor was no more inspiring, for I left a hot iron too long on a pair of pants, and so came to a humiliating conclusion with that job. When I was delivery boy for a druggist I dropped a filled bottle on the sidewalk and a policeman made me clean up the mess, while people looked on and laughed. This was too much for me, so I resigned, once more shamed into this foolish act

All these experiences, together with my background of poverty, gave me as fine an inferiority complex 'as a youngster ever started life with. It seemed that nothing ever could go right for me.

Then my grandmother, who next to my mother was dearest to me, died and I was ready to leave Salt Lake City and escape, perhaps, from a life which at best had been happy only in spots. I went to Chicago, where my father and older brother were then living, and though I was as green as an alfalfa field, I managed somehow to land a job. It was selling advertising for a religious paper, called World Wide Missions. Why they hired me, no one will ever know. They could not possibly have found a young man less suited to selling than I was at that time. Afraid of my own shadow, afraid of people, afraid of making mistakes, afraid of everything and sensitive as a magnolia flower. Just the slightest touch bruised my feelings.

The advertising manager of the paper was kind to me, giving me instructions on selling, and before long I was ready to make my first all. I went into the prospect's office, with my speech all ready. I had to sit there for an hour or more before I could see the man to whom I hoped to sell some space and all the time I was repeating to myself, "Young is my name, representing World Wide Missions," and then followed a line of talk which I hoped would be convincing. At last I was admitted to the man'$ office, and leaning against a table, I started my speech, but forgot everything except my name. The man looked at me in amazement, then his expression changed to one of kindliness and he helped me explain what paper I represented. But my troubles were just beginning, for when he asked the circulation of the paper I could not answer, and I did not even know whether it was a weekly or a monthly.

"Young man," said the prospect, "do you think you know enough to justify taking up my time? I suggest that hereafter you learn something about your job before going out to call on busy men."

My senses came back to me with a rush, and, deeply humiliated, I thanked my unknown friend for his advice and told him he was right.

"I'll never make that mistake again!" I promised him, but it was more a promise to myself than to him. He taught me a lesson that I have not forgotten. He did more than that, for he gave me an order. It turned out that he knew about my paper, and merely had asked me those questions to find out how much I knew. Out of the kindness of his heart he made my first call a success in every way, and I began then to learn that the average human being is very decent in his attitude toward young men just starting out. A thousand times I have tried to be as nice to others as that man was to me. In a way my adventure with him marked the beginning of a new phase of my new life.

After that I studied very hard, worked hard and began to have fair success in one selling job after another. Still, I was far from happy, and hadn't the faintest idea how happiness was to be achieved. The truth is, I set about finding it in the worst way possible, for I timed to fast living. In those days, as in these, salesmen often thought drinking a part of their work. I tried that, gave it a very earnest trial, and I know now that the drinking salesman is just plain foolish. It often helps land business for his house, but it will bring him down, and I don't care for any methods that result in the destruction of the individual. Yes, I know that men can drink a little and do themselves no great harm, but drinking is not a legitimate way to sell, and if a product or idea depends on liquor for its success, there is something wrong with it. A shrewd old Yankee is supposed to have said to his son: "My boy, honesty is the best policy. I know, for I have tried both." If I had a son I certainly would say to him: "My boy, sobriety is the best policy. I know, for I have tried both." Those drinking days were my drifting days, always in search of happiness, always hoping for a break, but never getting either. What a fool I was! Without stopping to think I threw away years of my life which might have been equally as happy as the past ten years have been. Once I sank so low in spirit and courage that I planned to have a look at the next life, in the belief that it could not be worse than this one and might be a whole lot better. Something, I don't know what, stopped me from any such retreat from a mess that was wholly of my own creation, and that could remedied at any time by my own efforts.

From Chicago I moved to New York, where, despite the turmoil and sourness inside of me, I managed to make a living while failing to make a life. As eastern advertising manager for a magazine I continued to disintegrate, until I began to see a light. Dimly at first, for I was a long, long way from the source of that light, which is just plain common sense. It had not occurred to me that my unhappiness was due to my own foolishness. I had not then come to see that happiness or unhappiness is largely a matter of choice. But I had made the start toward better things, for I had begun to analyze myself, and one day this idea popped into my mind:

"Suppose you owned a factory," I said to myself, "would you manufacture only stuff that you do not want, do not need and cannot use to advantage? Would you deliberately operate your factory in such a way as to make it definitely harmful to you, the owner? Well, then, consider that you do own a factory, a thought factory. It is inside you, and you are both owner and superintendent. Also night watchman and everything else. Nothing can happen in that factory without your approval. Nothing can go into it, neither raw materials nor partly manufactured goods, except on your permission. Nothing can come out of it except the products that you yourself design.

"A thought factory! That's what you have inside you," I said to myself, "and you have turned it into a producer of junk Take a look at your products. Fear, worry, impatience, anger, doubt. Are you proud of them? Can you expect other people to welcome such goods as you are manufacturing? Not a bit of it! Your factory is a menace to yourself and a nuisance to others,"

CHAPTER THREE
I GOT TIRED OF BEING A FOOL

THAT thought-factory idea did me worlds of good, but it alone was not sufficient to transform failure into success, and I was a gloomy failure still. I was eternally trying to get more out of life without putting more into it, with depressing results. My temper was ugly. I was going nowhere, for too much of my energy was devoted to the manufacture of sympathy for myself. It is a big job to retool a manufacturing plant. It cost Henry Ford a stack of millions to change from Model T to Model A, and I had to make a bigger change than that, but without enough capital to tide me over any shut-down period.

"What's the matter?" I asked myself, and kept on asking that same question, hoping that the answer some day would come. I prodded myself hard at this period of transition, and always there was the temptation to evade complete honesty. It is so easy—and so dangerous—to rationalize. It is equally easy—and equally dangerous—to become a martyr in one's own thinking. For day after day the battle raged within me before the forces of gloom began to give way. The trouble was that I lacked dominion over my own emotions and thoughts.

Dominion! That word stuck in my mind. I needed it. No man ever needed it more than I did. But how to acquire it? That was the rub. The products of my factory were a little improved, but not enough yet to please me, or to please others. I thought and I thought. I checked back over my life. I analyzed and re analyzed. I read, and I read some more, for I knew I was face to face with a crisis. From this time forth I was to disintegrate or to construct a life that was worth living. One night in my reading I came across a familiar passage in the Bible.

"The Kingdom of God is within you," said the passage. In other words, "The Kingdom of Heaven is within you." It had been saying that same thing for two thousand years, and it had been saying it to me for more than thirty years, but I had never given it much attention until I began to tire of my own futility. This night the passage seemed almost illuminated on the printed page. Its meaning struck me all of a sudden. " Why, that means me," I said to myself. "It means that my Kingdom of Heaven is within me,"

Obviously. Why hadn't I seen that before? A truth discovered always seems so plain and simple that we wonder why the discovery was so long delayed. I now that my factory was capable of taking the raw materials of experience, mingling them with faith, love and other qualities, and so becoming a plant worth operating, My next step was to make a list of the qualities that seemed to me ever-enduring, the qualities upon which the continuity of life depends, and without which life long since would have perished from the earth, perished in misery and in failure. These words seemed to me most worthy of places on my list: Love, Courage, Cheerfulness, Activity, Compassion, Friendliness, Generosity, Tolerance, Justice. Nine magic words! Perhaps in them was the secret of that Kingdom of Heaven I was seeking so earnestly.

Night after night I sat alone with these words,

fixing them in my consciousness, comprehending them, deciding what to do about them. Reflect them in my conduct, that's what I would do about them. They all are positive. They are dominant. They are stronger than their opposites. If they were weaker, life could not have advanced. Each represents a quality which has contributed to the progress of life in the mass, and it seemed to me quite evident that these same qualities would save an individual. My course, after that, was plain, though not easy. Live these words, these qualities! That was the way out of the darkness and muck in which I had been groping. But first I must get rid of the accumulation of disastrous junk my old factory had turned out.

It was at this time that I resigned my job. It was the time that old Vash Young died and left to me that inheritance I am talking about. First, I decided to cut out all habits which seemed to be harmful or even questionable. I listed my habits, and found that liquor, coffee, tea and tobacco all could be dispensed with, so within the space of a single day I cut these things out of my life. That wasn't so easy, either! You who are coffee drinkers know the depression, the anger, the petulance that comes when suddenly you find yourself without this stimulant, and you who use tobacco know the misery that comes when you leave off smoking for a few days. Theretofore I had battled these habits with my own will power, but it was always a losing fight Human will was not strong enough for such a battle. It took reason and understanding to win the day. I realized that these things were not a part of my Kingdom of Heaven. I saw that these desires were weak props for self-indulgence to Ian upon, and as my old self had faded out these things faded out also. Dominion over these habits was a great victory for me, and I have felt a wonderful sense of freedom ever since.

I started out on my career as an insurance salesman while still in the midst of this battle with physical habits, and at first business was dull. For a time my household was hard up, but very happy. Happier than we had ever been before, for we were fighting and winning a series of battles, one of which was to get rid of self'-centeredness. Whenever I'd find myself thinking of myself, I'd say, "Now is the time to think of somebody else, anybody else except myself!" There came a time when I was compelled to have some money. Our condition was desperate, and I almost slipped back into old mental channels, easy channels made wide and deep by long years of habit. I thought of a battle fought in Italy by Napoleon. The shooting was going against him, and one of his generals rode up and said, "It seems to me this is a battle lost!" But the Little Corporal replied hotly, ^e 'It seems to me a battle won!" And he did win it. But I'm no Napoleon. There is not even a touch of genius in me, not anything at all in me to distinguish me from the average man. So I wavered in this emergency, and had to check myself sharply. "When you are keenly conscious of your own needs, go out and do something for somebody else!" I demanded. "If you don't, you'll lose what ground you have gained." That seemed to be spiritually sound reasoning, so I tried it.

Over on the East Side in New York City there was a hospital for crippled children. I went to the superintendent and persuaded him to let me entertain the youngsters. I began by telling them stories, which fell flat. Next I tried reading to them, and that venture flopped also. I was up against it now for a fact, for here I had attempted to do something for somebody else and was about to fail in it. The crippled children would have been none the worse off for my failure, but it might have meant disaster for me, so in desperation I decided that on my next visit to the hospital I'd sing. Now, I'm no wood thrush. As a singer, I rank closer to the jaybird, but the children liked my singing.

Every Sunday for a year I went to that hospital and sang. I know nothing of music, so to keep my repertoire fresh, I'd get talking- machine records, play them on the machine at home, and in that way learn the songs. At the outset I did not have money enough to pay for the records, but when I explained to the recording company what I was doing, they gave me fifty songs for children, all of which I learned by painstaking practice over the music-box in our little apartment. But before that year was over I had money enough to buy records, and to buy many other things, too. By refusing to put money first, I seemed to have hit on a profitable program. And by profit I mean happiness.

I determined years ago never to undertake any business venture if my happiness would be in the least disturbed in case it failed. Before I called on any prospect for insurance, I checked up on my own mental processes, to make sure that I would not be cast down if he refused to buy. This doesn't mean that I shy off from any solicitation, either; it merely means that before I make the call I get myself into the right frame of mind.

One time I was working on a very large policy and had spent much time and money in preparation of the case. I had not then become prosperous, but this case would have landed me on Easy Street for a while.

The morning came for me to close the contract, and I set out for the man's office. This was such an important occasion for me that on the way I found a quiet place, and stopped, physically and mentally, to be sure that I was not riding for a fall. "Will I be downcast if this man fails to come across?" I asked, and at first the answer wasn't quite dear, whereupon I decided to ditch the whole venture rather than lose my battle with myself. But this very decision won the battle for me, so I was free to proceed according to plan.

The man saw me as soon as I sent in my name. We began to talk, and he steered the conversation away from the subject of insurance. I saw then that the policy I had worked so hard to land was all but lost. The man became apologetic "I feel miserable about this," he said. "You had good reason to think I would take out this insurance, and you have spent much time and money trying to sell me, but I can't go through with it..."

"Now you forget all about me," I broke in. Q 'I came here to do you a service, and I see I am making you unhappy. I'm not worried over your refusal to buy insurance, but I am worried because you are worrying. I have had some good times talking with you, and that's pay a-plenty. Let's call it a day, and don't you give another thought to the subject."

I left his office in higher spirits than I. had known on entering it. Once again I had proved my dominion over disappointment, and as this was early in my new career, that meant worlds tome. It was victory of the sweetest kind. The incident was of vast value in my own regeneration.

A few weeks passed, and then a letter came from this man, asking me to call again, which I did.

" I still cannot take out that insurance," he said, "but I have been wondering if you could use letters of introduction to one hundred of the biggest men in New York. You were so decent to me that I want to make it up to you. Besides, an insurance agent who does not put on the pressure is so rare that I'd like some of my friends to meet you."

Could I use one hundred personal letters from a business leader to other business leaders! Well, I certainly could, and every one of those letters was written by this man for me. They gave me a working program for an entire year. They re- suited in many times more insurance written by me than I possibly could have written for this one prospect, and they proved all over again that this fortune I had inherited was worth something in the world of business.

My dominion over disappointment was by now fairly well entrenched, but I had not quite licked bad temper. I needed an adventure to prove my dominion over that, and it came, all right. A trivial thing it was, but worth millions to me in happiness. We were living then away out in the Bronx, and one night I had remained down-town in Manhattan until a very late hour. Subway trains were running at infrequent intervals. I was dog-tired, eager to be home and in bed. I dived into a subway hole, hoping to play in luck and get a train within a minute or two, and there was a train standing in the station, its doors wide open. I bolted for a door, but the guard slid it shut in my very face. He saw me coming. He knew there would not be another train for perhaps ten or fifteen minutes, and he could have admitted me just as easily as he excluded me. His act was unnecessarily rude, and I felt a hot wave of anger sweep over me. In true New York fashion I started to yell at him but then I stopped.

" Don't be a fool!" I said to myself. 'You've missed the train, and nothing you can do will enable you to make it now. You've got to wait until the next one comes along. Why burn up what little energy you have left by getting mad?"

The reasoning was sound, but reasoning is never enough in my use. It must be followed by action, and this night I was very conscious that my reasoning had not won a complete victory. I still was hot under the collar, so I began to wonder what I could do to get rid of that miserable feeling. Looking around I saw a woman with a baby and a suitcase. She was just leaving the station.

"May I help you?" I asked, " I need help," she replied, "but I'm afraid it would be an imposition on you to come with me, for I am going across town to the Pennsylvania station."

"Let me take you," I urged, and grabbing her To suitcase we went back to the street, where I hailed a cab and we drove over to her destination. I waited there until her train was ready, helped her aboard, and again started home, two hours after I had missed that subway train. But I was in high spirits, for I had put myself through a course of discipline, had conquered a silly fit of temper by doing something for somebody else. My fatigue was gone, and I was very happy.

I hope you will believe me when I say that these incidents are related in no self-righteous or boastful spirit. I tell them humbly to illustrate the manner in which I gained such dominion as I have over my own weakness. There is no other way in which I can share my fortune except by a delineation of each victory that I have been fortunate enough to win. Many others have won similar victories, and still others need to win them. Only recently I saw a man ruin his day by giving in to an insane attack of futile anger. He had left his home to drive to a suburban station, but just as his car got to the road in front of his house, it stopped. He jumped out, looked at his watch, swore mightily and then began jerking at various things under the hood of that car. Nothing he did had any effect upon the machine, for the gasoline tank was empty, as he soon discovered. This infuriated him still more, and he called hotly to his wife to know why she had used up all the gas and not told him about it. His swearing became very red, for he was about to miss his train and he had an engagement in New York which, he said, was at nine o'clock. doubt very much if that was true, for not many New York engagements are made for such an early hour.

A bus came along and the irate commuter hopped into it. The bus moved slowly down the street, and the commuter sat there, tense in every muscle, his watch in his hand, swearing under his breath. There was nothing in the world he could do that would make traffic open and so speed the bus to the station. But he shoved hard on the seat ahead of him, his face became almost purple, and he denounced everything he could think of. He made his train, but he might as well have at home, for his day was ruined before it had begun. That unwise man, lacking utterly any control over his own emotions, burned up enough energy within twenty minutes to have landed several big con ᵉ tracts for him. Burned it up to no purpose in the world. He was either going to make that train, or he was going to miss it. He might as well have been pleasant it, and thus have saved himself a little stress and strain. As 1 0b' served this incident I realized with a surge of shame that before I became tired of being a fool I was guilty of many such explosions of intelligence.

Life becomes almost automatic once you have tapped the sources of strength, of love, of happiness upon which life depends. It is silly for a poor insignificant mortal, such as I am, to buck the stream of life. I sought out its current and try to flow along with it. That stream is impelled by the nine qualities I listed earlier in this chapter, and it is the fortune these qualities have brought me that I'd like to share, and feel obligated to share with all others.

CHAPTER FOUR

PHANTOMS AND SCARECROWS

No MAN ever had a harder fight against fear than I have had. Most people are afraid of something, but I was afraid of almost everything, including mice. My mother had an inordinate dread of these little beasts, and I sup, pose I acquired the fear from observing her. And thunder-storms! What a terror they were to me when I was a child. In those days a great many persons dreaded thunder-storms as a sort of scourge. They seemed to think that behind the flashing of lightning, the roaring and rumbling of thunder there was a terrific and pagan god run amuck, determined in his fury to destroy petty creatures who dared to walk the earth. When a thunder-storm came in the daylight hours, the family huddled in a tightly dosed room, where the air soon became oppressive, but no one was bold enough to open a door or window. At night the situation was even worse, for darkness, to a man afraid, usually adds another element to his terror. Many a night I have buried my head in the bedding and tried to shut out the dreadful noise of a harmless thunder-storm.

When I was a youngster out in Salt Lake City I used to dread the opening of school, for I was afraid to meet new teachers, and afraid of new toughs who had moved into the neighborhood since the last session ended. In the classrooms I was a timid soul, answering hesitantly when called on. One day as I was leaving school to go home for my lunch an older boy pointed out an imaginary figure of a man hidden in a tree beside my path. He suggested that this man was there to grab me. In my mind I suppose I knew this was foolish, but my emotions were too strong for my reasoning in those days, and though I was terribly hungry, I remained at school throughout the lunch hour, and did not get up nerve to go home until long after the school had closed for the day.

I dreaded physical combats, and those were the days of fights. The present-day boy has no real concept of the barbarity which was common among boys of twenty years ago. There were kid gangs in every town, and a member of one gang dared not go into territory claimed by a rival gang. The fighting usually was done with sticks and stones. Several of my friends have scars on them-now as a result of these kid fights which, for some reason, our elders seemed to think natural. Cops used to chase us sometimes, but no others ever interfered with our warfare unless a stone went wild and broke a window. Cops were bitter enemies of boys twenty years ago. Sometimes I think the greatest advance made by society within our generation is the new attitude toward children as exhibited in efforts to direct play, and to inculcate the ideals of Boy and Girl Scouts into youngsters.

Unavoidably I was caught in some fights, and when my temper became sufficiently aroused, I could and did fight recklessly. But I ducked as many combats as I could. One instance I recall now with particular shame. Somehow, I was chosen captain of a gang, and war was brewing with a rival gang. As captain I should have been the actual leader in combat, but I persuaded my gang that a captain's duty was to direct, not to participate. When the first battle of this juvenile war came on, I watched my fellows go to it, while I remained on the side-lines, "directing."

Stage fright was also one of my tormentors. In our school plays I should have found great fun; instead, I found nothing but worry. For days before the big nights I went around with a sick and sinking feeling in my stomach. I shall never forget one play in which I had the lead. I had to sing a song with a high note in it. In rehearsals I managed to get by, high note and all, but when the day for the performance arrived I was a wreck. Defeated before the thing began. A pathetic little coward into whose life fear had been allowed to grow as a dominant influence. On that fateful night I started off well enough with my part, but when I reached the dreaded song with the high note, my voice just broke and faded out completely. I fled from the stage, and no amount of coaxing could get me back. In my own eyes I was permanently disgraced. At that moment, and for days afterward, life did not seem to me worth living. My best girl was playing opposite me in the play, and she would have nothing to do with me after my ignominious retreat. This added to the burden of disgrace. As I walked along the streets, which I did as little as possible, I imagined that people were turning to look at me, and when I heard someone laugh I was sure he was laughing at me. Shivers ran up and down my back. My face flushed. I suffered agony as only a boy an suffer when he thinks himself disgraced. But no one took me aside and braced me up. These adventures with fear also were considered a part of my nature.

As a young man my fears remained with me. When I had to approach an employer on some matter of business my voice always was unsteady and my knees more so. If it were possible to draw a chart of my impulses in those days, the chart would show a steadily falling line going in the direction of some humble hiding-place. My emotions directed that I hide from life, from failure. As I look back now I am certain these inward quaking's caused me to try liquor. It provided a fool's escape from himself—for a few moments.

Some time ago I sat opposite a man in the New York subway. When he came in his face was sagging, presenting a clear picture of his feelings. In a few minutes he began to change his expression. First he held his mouth in a firm line, then he clenched his fists and looked defiantly about him. Poor fellow, I know what was wrong with him. He was a salesman working up his courage to tackle a tough prospect. He dreaded his job, but he had to go through with it, and before he came to his destination on the subway, he was a pretty fair imitation of a brave looking man. But he wasn't brave. Down inside him were quivers and quakes. The food he had eaten at lunch could not possibly have been assimilated, for all his energy and all the processes of his body were directed toward the building up of a false front. The most profane man I know is profane because he dislikes his real timid self, and has created this other boisterous, swearing, swashbuckling individual to substitute for him.

For such persons I have the deepest sympathy. I have been there.

There is not a doubt nor a dread nor a sick sensation I have not had. In my early days as a salesman of advertising I often have become so nauseated as I contemplated my next call that I lost my food in the gutter. Literally, that is true. Not once, but time after time I have had this wretched experience, due always to fear. I have prayed—how I have prayed!— that the prospect would be out of his office when I got there.

In sales meetings I sat there dreading to be called on. My heart would start pumping like a fire-engine when I saw the boss looking at me, and my breath would come in gasps. I could not make even a simple statement without going through minutes of agony.

The best business opportunity I had as a young man I lost through fear. An elderly man had taken an interest in me. Probably he, too, as a youngster, had been afraid, and he recognized the symptoms in me. He knew that he had mastered the false feeling, and guessed that I could be led to do the same thing. Anyway, he offered to take me in as a partner on a very small salary, but with a liberal commission on sales. I accepted, but before the sun had set that day I began to doubt. What if I did not make any sales? What if I became sick, and so could not earn commissions? What if the business went broke? What if the senior partner died before I could establish myself? These are just a few of the "what ifs" which plagued me. In the end, I ran out on that offer and lived to see another youngster step into the place I had retreated from and within a few years make a splendid thing of the opportunity.

After many years of vain struggling against fear, I began to think about that thought factory inside myself. Why was I letting it manufacture so much fear? I didn't want that product. Nobody wanted it. Wasn't I the owner and the superintendent of that factory? Then why not turn out something worth-while?

I had reached the grand crisis of my life. Fortunately, I knew this. Recognized it with absolute certainty. But what was I to do? First of all I decided that I must do something to vanquish fear. The thing I feared most was failure, loss of my job, loss of money and all the evils that go along with no income. This being my greatest fear at the moment, I decided that the only thing to do was to fail! Quit the job with nothing saved. Walk out on the streets with nothing to do, as I always had feared I might. Take a chance on to-morrow. In short, call the bluff of this great bully, fear.

That was strong medicine! But I needed strong medicine and had the sense to take it. I had to lick my fears, and I could not do it if I compromised on a single point. Deliberately I had brought about the condition which I most feared, but I found not one trace of fear in my feelings, only elation, romance, joy at a new start in a new world. But I still had a long way to go before victory became a habit.

I was told that "cold canvassing" was necessary if I wished to develop. This means calling on strangers without having made appointments and without even knowing anything of them. I dreaded this ordeal, but drove myself into it. First I selected the building which I thought good for the experiment, and going to the directory selected half a dozen names almost at random. I boarded an elevator and went to the floor of my first name, found the man's office, then turned and hurried to the elevator and went back into the streets, a defeated salesman. I walked heavily for a block or two, my mind a complete mess, my muscles weak, and with a feeling of nausea suggesting that once again I was about to suffer the final humiliation, loss of food in the gutter, not from illness, but from fear. But somehow, I was a little stronger this day than I had been. I stopped and spoke aloud to myself. "You miserable coward!" I said. "You set out to do a job and you crawl out on it. You will never get anywhere by bowing down this way to fear. Go on back and see those men!" I retraced my steps, called on every one of the men I had intended to call on, had some delightful talks with them and went home happy.

There were days and weeks and months, as I have told you, when I was hard up. Harmful mental habits and emotional weaknesses did not vanish overnight. They had to be chased out, but I had them on the run from the very minute I got up enough nerve to quit my old job and strike out afresh. Every engagement I have fought with these enemies since that day has been a rear-guard action. Now and then one of them has turned to snipe at me, but when I fired back the fight was over. A great victory almost always makes subsequent victories easy.

All my life I had feared to-morrow, until I decided to have faith and to live to-day in courage. "To-day is the to-morrow I worried about yesterday and it never happened," is the way someone has expressed my own feelings about to-day and to-morrow. There is nothing I can do about yesterday. To-morrow never comes. I am responsible only for to-day. That is my philosophy of time, and it has helped me out of many holes.

This subject of fear is a favorite of mine. Fear was my greatest enemy, and I am inclined to believe it is the greatest enemy of most other persons. Every friend I have has lost something because of fear, happiness if nothing more. Recently I asked twenty able men to describe their greatest fears. Five said poverty is the thing they dread most; three are afraid of disgrace in one form or another; one of high places; one of fire; two of sickness; one of doctors and physical examinations; one of being called on to speak in public; one of the dark; two of water, one of automobile accidents, and one of snakes.

In all this list there is not a fear that has a right to exist. These men are letting bogus feelings impair their happiness and their usefulness. It is nothing but common sense to be careful, and to work diligently against failure and poverty, but what good does it do to fear these things? Poverty never yet was chased away by fear. Work, thrift, faith and courage are the preventives of poverty, not fear. Dread of disgrace on the part of upright men is pure folly, for no disgrace can come to them unless they let it come. Honest failure certainly is no disgrace, and no one so regards it except the unfortunate person who has failed and permits himself to become a victim of a false interpretation of his own ill fortune. The attitude of all worth-while persons toward one who, through no fault of his own, has failed, is sympathetic, rather than condemnatory. This thing of fear, I tell you, is nothing in the world except a giving in by the person afraid to a feeling that has no right to exist. But it does exist on all sides. Go into your library some time and see how many books are listed under the heading of fear. Read biographies and you encounter frequent accounts of combats with fear, and of victories over it, for men about whom biographies are written usually are those who have overcome this emotion, who have thrust it out of their lives and substituted for it something that does them and others good service.

Select a hundred of your acquaintances at random and talk with as many of them as possible about opportunities they have muffed. Almost always the man speaking will say that he had at least one chance to make good in a big way, but that he lacked courage at the critical moment. "If I'd only had the nerve to go through with that deal, I'd be on Easy Street right now," is a sentence I have heard over and over again. Very few persons go through life without at least one big chance. fact that so many do not grasp it is due more often to fear than to any other one thing. Since the panic of 1929 the newspapers, magazines and books have been crowded with statements urging that we have courage. There are not many points upon which all men agree, but the need for courage is one of them, and all of our leaders can't be wrong all of the time. "Never strike sail to a fear," says Emerson, and every other man who has occupied a commanding position has said the same thing in one form or another. The coward is never admired, never held up as an ideal for anybody, so it must be that cowardice, or fear, is something to be shunned.

Every year we read of hunters and other adventurers in the great woods of the North who become lost. They say there is no other internal panic the equal of that which seizes a man when he loses his sense of direction. Sometimes he will run until his strength is all gone. Again he will walk in a circle. If he has a gun and ammunition he frequently discharges all his shots before any one knows he is lost, and so has no means of guiding a searching party to him. Obviously, the best thing for a man who is lost is calmness, but calmness is the first thing he loses. I once asked a great hunter about this terrible fear of being lost in some unmarked wilderness, and he replied he had never known that sensation, though there had been many occasions upon which he did not know where he was.

"When I realize that I do not know where I am," he said, "my first act is to think of something else. I know if I permit fear to creep into my thoughts, if I doubt my own ability to get back to base, I am in for trouble. So, I think of something else, of anything else, and somehow I have always found my way out. On one occasion I had gone with a friend into a forest that was completely unknown to us. We became tired of carrying our packs, so put them down, and went on with nothing but our guns. This was far in the North, where moss covers the earth, and we figured we could find our own trail in the moss, in case we did lose our direction. But after we had gone several miles a snow-storm suddenly came on, and within a few minutes it had obliterated any trail we had left. Also, it made every foot of earth look like every other foot. My friend began to show alarm. He was on the verge of panic and began to put doubt in my own mind until I spoke sharply to him, telling him to keep his mouth shut if he could talk of nothing better than freezing to death out there in the wilderness. But he was hard to quiet, for he was new to this game of hunting in the Arctic and had read too many stories of the tragedies which sometimes overtake men who go without guides into strange territory. Finally, however, I made him talk with me about other subjects. I had faith in my own instinct for direction, and that instinct I knew would save us unless we permitted it to be superseded by fear.

" We struck out in one direction, which so far as he could tell was the same as any other direction. But I was not afraid. I was letting my mind work for me instead of against me, and I figured my mind ought to be as good as that of an Indian or an animal, and neither Indians nor animals become lost. Mile after mile we trudged along, getting pretty cold and saying less and less to each other. Still I was confident, and not long after dark we came to our temporary camp. My friend was overjoyed and amazed and wanted to know how I had accomplished such a miracle, or how I had hit on such a lucky direction. But it was neither a miracle, nor was it luck, for I have done the same thing on other occasions by excluding from my mind the impulses and emotions which would have meant ruin."

We human beings have a lot of mental power which we do not realize. The trouble is that we destroy that power by letting fear and panic dethrone the normal and proper functioning of our intellects.

"I know you are right when you condemn fear," said a man to me, "but how am I to overcome it?"

The answer is, to take a fresh view of life. When a fear tries to creep into your thoughts, analyze it and see if there is good ground for it. The chances are a hundred to one that the fear is of something which has not yet happened, nor even begun to happen. It is imaginary trouble manufactured in your own thought factory, and you are perfectly able to shut down on that product and substitute another for it. Since the world began there has been fear, but this does not mean it is either necessary or intelligent. There has been meanness, too, ever since the world began, but that does not make it a required part of our equipment for life. Even if you take a materialistic view of existence, and believe only in the survival of the fittest, you are bound to see that most survivals are due to ability to overcome dangers, as well as fleetness in avoiding them.

A few years ago, it was the fashion when young folks gathered around a fire for a winter party to tell ghost stories and other stories of fear. "The scariest I ever was," a narrator would begin, and then relate a story of terror in which the fear was, almost always, without foundation. One story I recall was told by a man who was afraid of the dark and who thought he heard a wild animal calling in the woods near his house. He was certain it was a mountain lion, and so afraid was he that he broke out in a cold sweat. That man knew that mountain lions, except in a very few instances, have never been known to attack human beings. They will run from a man, or from a dog, but this man was none the less terrified, and so was his wife. He had no weapon with him that night, but he was unwilling to appear frightened before his wife, partly because of pride and partly because he did not wish to increase her alarm. Finally, he said, it became spiritually necessary for him to walk outside and examine the premises, which he proceeded to do with a flash-light.

" I was so scared," he said, " that I felt as light as air. If a mountain lion had sprung at me I could have sprung right out of his way. He wouldn't have had a chance either in a foot-race or a jumping contest with me that night. I looked everywhere except in one clump of bushes, driving myself to the search and dreading more than anything else that clump of shrubbery. I started to go indoors again without looking there, but something made me give up that plan. I had started out to conquer my own fear of the dark, and to prove to my wife that I was not afraid, and I had to go through with it.

Over toward the bushes I went, walking very softly and very, very gingerly. I flashed my light into the undergrowth, stood still for a moment and then felt a long soft body rub against the back of my legs. Without effort I rose into the air, autogiro fashion, only I got off to a better start than any machine ever will. When I landed again after several seconds of floating, my light fell full upon a startled house cat, who streaked away for the bam as fast as she could go. I came back into my house feeling foolish, and I was foolish, for there had been no animal bigger than a pussy-cat near my house. Still, I'm glad of the experience, for I have not been so afraid of the dark since that cat caused me to defy the law of gravity."

That is a typical fear story. Usually the thing we dread is a house cat and not a lion. The prospect whom salesmen dread turns out to be a man who is ruled by his wife. The energy spent in steeling ourselves for the call is spent uselessly for there is nothing to be afraid of. When I began my combat with fear I knew there was an inexhaustible supply of imaginary fear upon which I might draw, and an equally large supply of courage. I could look them over and take my choice. Any one, seeing the situation in this light, would choose courage, or faith, or affirmative thinking, or belief in God or whatever you choose to call the force that enables life to go forward.

When I was a boy farmer used scarecrows in their fields. Many timid birds, seeing the flapping of a ragged pair of pants, an old coat and a hat all hung on crossed sticks, would fly away, but now and then a wiser bird would come down and enjoy a feast, using the scarecrow as a perch between meals. I thought very little of the significance of the thing at that time, but since I became tired of being a fool, it has occurred to me time and again that the fears of life are nothing more than scarecrows. Realiza-

tion of this is the heart of that fortune I inherited, and I'd rather share
this realization with you than any other,

The conquest of fear is one continuous grand and glorious feeling!

CHAPTER FIVE
ARE YOU WORKNG FOR THE WRONG BOSS?

WITHIN the past few years hundreds of salesmen have come to me with their troubles. Things are going badly at home. Business is sour. They are in debt. Office politics is against them. Competition is keen and unfair. Selling is a rotten job, anyway. And a whole lot more.

"Do you think of these things in business hours?" I ask.

"Can't think of anything else," is the usual reply.

No wonder business is bad for men whose minds have run amuck in this fashion. Those who go about, drawing pay from others, but giving their thoughts to their own private, selfish troubled situations are fore-doomed to disappointing results. The only way to get business is to think of the prospect's needs, of the company's needs, and to reflect positive, admirable qualities in your own conduct. Most of us reap exactly what we sow, and if we go about sowing nothing but trouble, the harvest is bound to be more trouble. Wheat never yet grew from Canada thistle seed.

Salesmen, as a class, are a loyal bunch, but the greatest excuse-makers under the sun. They are not entirely to blame for this alibi habit. Sales managers are a hard driving lot. Pressure selling is firmly rooted in American economic life, and I'm sorry it is, for it should not be necessary. Some people think part of the panic following 1929 was due to too much pressure in selling. Whether this is true or not I cannot say, and it is not my intention to go further into an analysis of the panic. My ideas, such as they are, are all for the individual.

I know what it is to go out and pound the pavements for days on end without getting an order. Like most other salesmen, I have walked around the block many times trying to get up nerve to go on in and tackle a prospect, and I often have been delighted when that prospect was out of the office. It was better still if he was out of town, for this excuse would have to be accepted by my employers. I have loafed away valuable hours in motion-picture houses. I have kidded myself into thinking that Monday was a bad day because business men have not yet recovered from the week-end, and that Friday was a bad day because they were thinking of the next week-end. All of this junk is standard equipment in many a salesman's mind.

A friend of mine who was not doing so well finally gave me his working habits. He never tried to make an appointment before ten in the morning, because he thought the prospect would be busy opening mail until that hour. He never tried to do anything between twelve and two-thirty, as that was lunch time, and he never attempted a sale after four, for fear the prospect's mind would be relaxed, and his thoughts turning to the quitting hour. Out of an eight-hour day this man was working but three and a half. The remainder of the time he was stalling and kidding himself into thinking all his stalling was wise.

When I became an insurance salesman, which was at the time I inherited my fortune of affirmative thinking, I determined to work out a system of my own. I knew from personal experience, and from listening to many conversations, that insurance agents were dreaded above all other salesmen. For many years the insurance companies were careless about the personnel of their agents. Any old bore would do provided he could sell a few policies. That was in the day when insurance was sold by telling the prospect of the imminence of death. There were a lot of stock stories about men who had wanted to take out large policies, but had put off the decision for a few days, and then either died or contracted incurable ailments before the contract was closed. Gee! What killjoys some of the old-time insurance salesmen were! If insurance had not been socially and economically sound, its early salesmen would have killed the business. All of us recall those awful old-time salesmen, and once in a while we encounter a survivor of the gloom school of insurance selling. Crapehangers. Grave-diggers. Prophets of evil. I shudder now to think of them.

Yet, I owe them something, for I learned from them how not to sell. I make it easy, always, for the man on whom I am calling to get rid of me. When I go into a prospect's office I do not sit down, even if he has invited me to, until I have told him what my mission is. If he is interested, I remain; if not, there is no embarrassment to him or to me. That's the approach I have found most effective. No shoving of the foot into the door, no pulling up of a chair close to the prospect, no leaning over his desk and breathing foul cigar smoke into his face, no beating about the bush at all. Just a plain simple approach, as one gentleman to another. Perhaps as a result of this technique, which I do not regard as technique by the way, I am never at a loss for additional prospects. My friends keep me supplied with many more names than I can use, and I could get a bushel of letters of introduction any time I asked for them.

The next thing after getting a man's interest, is to figure about how much to offer him. Here, again, my plan differs radically from the standard plan of selling. I always submit a policy smaller than I think the man should take out, and let him raise it. That makes him feel comfortable, whereas if I submitted him a large policy and he had to cut down the figure, he might feel a little uncomfortable. My idea always is to make the man on whom I call glad that I came to see him. This I do as a matter of ethics, not primarily as a business matter, but it is good business, just the same. A salesman who strikes for one sale and no subsequent sales, is silly. When I sell a prospect, I hope to sell him more later on, if he wishes, and if he does not wish, I hope he will feel free to recommend me to some of his friends. All of this, you may say, is pretty dose to shrewd selfishness, or self-interest. It can be so interpreted, but that is not the correct interpretation, for my actual thought is of the prospect's comfort. It is just a fine break of life that in some cases business follows in the wake of considerate conduct.

The biggest thing in selling is not the method, however, but the mental attitude. When I was selling newspaper advertising space one of my fellow workers came in one day and, going up to the boss, said:

"I want you to go out with me to-morrow."

What for?" asked the boss.

"Because I want to prove to you that there is not a line of business to be had in my territory!" No, all poor salesmen are not gone yet. Within the past few weeks I have heard of several who are doing the calling no good at all. Here's the star example of unwise, immoral, profitless approaches:

At school commencement season last year a prominent New York scientist received a telephone call from an insistent stranger.

" Are you the father of the young man graduated yesterday from Such-and-Such a school?" asked the voice on the telephone. "Yes," replied the scientist.

" Then I think you'll want to see me right away. It is something important concerning your boy, and I can't speak of it over the phone."

Of course the agitated father told him to come right down. He then called up his own home, and his wife did not know where their son was at the moment. He had gone out, she said. Half an hour of agonized suspense followed for the father, and then the mysterious stranger appeared.

" What about my boy?" demanded the scientist.

" What has happened to him? Where is he?"

" Why, nothing has happened to him, so far as I know," said the stranger. "I came to see you about giving him a life-insurance policy for a graduating present."

The scientist did not kick that solicitor out, as he should have done. Instead, he had him sit there while he told him something of the ways of business and of gentlemen. Naturally, he bought no insurance from that fellow.

A close friend of mine told me a story almost as bad as that. He had for years run a charge account at a fashionable clothing store, and one day he took an acquaintance, who wanted a suit of clothes, into that establishment. They looked around, selected a suit and the acquaintance asked whether or not there were two pairs of trousers with it.

" Our clients," said the haughty clerk, "would not be interested in a second pair of trousers."

"Then will you tell me whether or not this suit is durable?"

"Sorry," offered the clerk, "but we rarely pay any attention to durability, as our clientele is interested in appearance, and not especially in longevity of clothing."

The two men left that store, and not one of them has spent a cent there since. What selling! Here was a salesman trying to make a prospect feel small. But that was just before the depression. No doubt there is a different atmosphere there now. Depressions are not wholly useless if they result in unemployment for salesmen like that.

Such bizarre examples as these two are rare, I hope. But bad selling is far from rare. Every one of us meets with it every week. Some time ago a woman came into my office with some window ventilators for sale. I was very busy and told her I did not want any ventilators. When she turned to go out, I saw such a tragic look come over her face that I called her back and asked her what was wrong. She explained that her husband, formerly a man of means, had lost his business, and that she had gone out to work in the hope of helping provide for their four children. I bought two ventilators from her, and then told her how to sell some more. First, I convinced her that the article she was selling had real value, and that she should, therefore, call on prospects with the conviction that she could render them a service. Also, I urged that she put her home situation out of her mind, if possible, while selling, and that instead of dejection, she try to radiate good humor and cheer. I then gave her a list of men on whom she might call and told her that they needed window ventilators to protect them from cold breezes in winter, and dust and dirt in summer. She went out and began making sales.

Within a few days her husband called to see me, and he, too, was deep in gloom.

" I've been unemployed a long time," he said, "and our situation is desperate. But for the bravery and ability of my wife, we'd be sunk."

"You are doing plenty of work," I said to him, "but you are working for the wrong boss. Your boss is Old Man Gloom. I'd quit him, if I were you, and work for Mr. Hope."

We had a long talk, and he got the idea I was trying to put over to him. When he got a good job later and his wife was able to go back to homemaking they thought a sort of miracle had happened to them, but the only thing that had happened was a change of mental attitude. In selling, in life itself, the state of mind is the big thing. The worst competitor any salesman has to deal with is his own mental attitude.

Once an actor came to see me. He had been "at liberty," as actors call unemployment, for much too long, and was then engaged in trying to sell ginger ale to grocery stores. That was mean work for an actor. I tried to show him that his attitude toward his temporary job was all wrong.

"But what can a man do," he asked, " when he is selling something that does not seem to him a necessity? The world could get along without ginger ale, you know, even though it is a good drink, and a lot of people make their living out of it."

"If you take that attitude," I replied, "there is but one thing for you to do, and that is to sell yourself. Decide on the qualities which seem to you most worth-while, and then go out to reflect those qualities in your contact with others. What are the qualities you admire most?"

Together we made a list, and in it were cheerfulness, courage, interest in others, and so on, He decided to try this method out a while. It brought him some ray of happiness and hope, enough to last until he returned to the stage.

This case seems to me very important, for it illustrates a mental condition I often encounter. I should explain again that all these incidents are known to me because I give over one day each week to people who are in trouble. Those who have come to me tell others, and my friends send many of their troubled callers to me. I am glad to see them all. My inheritance, as I have said, required that I do everything possible for my fellow humans, and nothing gives me a greater thrill than to see some downcast man or woman take a new look at life, and go forth to fight a battle and win a victory over negative thinking.

Sometimes one line of reasoning and sometimes another is effective, and sometimes I fail to do any good at all. But I try. I have made it a rule these past ten successful years to devote less than half of my time to my own affairs. I must earn a living, but I need happiness as much as I need food and shelter, and a considerable part of my happiness comes from these extra-official duties. I rarely am asked to give money to any troubled caller, for it is not money he needs so much as it is an affirmative attitude toward life. It is a view-point which brings happiness that I have to share.

But I was talking of selling. Sometimes I wish I were a sales manager. I'd like to be one just for a week or so. Just long enough to write one letter to all of my salesmen. Sales managers write many letters. Pep letters. Go-getter letters. Confidence letters. Letters full of drive. Packed with forceful expressio "Bull letters," the boys call them. Salesmen are not such hero worshipers as they pretend to be when in the presence of their bosses. Here's the letter I'd send out to my salesmen:

"Dear Mr. Blank:

"Your reports recently have been a disappointment. Our competitors in your district are enjoying a big business in orders, while your orders are falling off. Our product is right, our prices are right, and our advertising is intelligent. The trouble, therefore, must be with you. I have given your case careful thought, and have decided to rescind all previous instructions, and issue in place of them the following fifteen things you must do:

"1. Get up in the morning and start thinking of yourself.

"2. If things don't go just right at home be sure to get in a couple of nasty digs at someone before leaving the house.

"3. If it is a rainy day, kick about the weather and let it interfere with your work ^{cc} 4. Don't be pleasant when you go into the office.

"5. If you hear of a big order going through, label its luck for the other fellow and be envious of him, instead of trying to learn something from it that will help you.

"6. Sit in your office and plan your work during the golden hours you should be in your prospect's office.

"7. Do the easy, non-productive things to-day and kid yourself into thinking that you will get down to work to-morrow.

"8. Plan your work so that if you miss a few calls to-day you will be left stranded high and dry until to-morrow.

"9. If you get an order be satisfied, go out and celebrate, and then a while before trying for another.

"10. If you are ahead of your quota, take it easy.

" 11. If you are behind, give up entirely, and then start over again next month when your next quota period sets in.

" 12. Convince yourself that your territory is not so good as the other fellow's.

"13. Give in to that ^C lot down' feeling after eating too much lunch.

"14. Don't waste any time studying the business.

"15. Enlist all your thinking against you instead of in your favor.

"Yours for the Company,

" Vash Young."

Some such letter as that would ridicule a salesman out of the foolish non-productive methods all too frequently engaged in.

CHAPTER SIX

THE PERVERSITY OF HUMAN NATURE

I SOMETIMES think if that famous tree in the Garden of Eden had carried a sign saying "Take One," the whole history of the human race would have been different. And I sometimes think that if the government ordered every person to drink liquor, we might have more sobriety. For human nature is a curious thing, often rebelling against orders and prohibitions. I am certain that if some power should order each of us to go out and be a fool, most of us would resent that instruction so much that we would be wise in our conduct.

Suppose, for example, someone ordered you to get up in an ugly mood each morning, make your wife and children unhappy by outbursts of temper at breakfast, and then take with you to the office a grouch so heavy that you could get no work done until noon? Suppose someone ordered you to smoke too much, drink harmfully, eat too much, sleep too little, and do various other things all of which you know would cut down your happiness and your income, would you submit? Not for a single day! Yet many of us do these very things. Make a list of the silly things you have done within the past week, and then ponder that list for a few minutes. Would you have done any one of those things if someone had told you it was required? I doubt it. A prominent man of my acquaintance says that he was cured of drinking by his wife, who told him that he simply must get drunk and make a disgusting fool of himself every Thursday. He had no intention whatever of yielding to any such instruction, but if she had been less wise, he might have been that fool she told him he must be.

A very close friend of mine who lives an hour's ride from New York has a temperamental furnace in his airy country house. That furnace has a way of going out at the most inopportune moments. On several occasions last winter when my friend and his wife remained in New York for a theater party, he found the fire all gone when he reached his home in the wee hours. Now that's a bad time to find a furnace gone dead on you. If you leave it alone, the pipes may freeze before moving, and that may mean a plumbing bill mounting into the hundreds of dollars. If, on the other hand, you attempt to start the fire again, that requires at least one hour's work, for hard coal is a slow starter, as every furnace-tender knows.

It was my friend's custom, when he found the fire out, to storm and rage, kick the furnace, cuss the suburbs and in general destroy all the good effects of an otherwise pleasant evening. Incidentally, he would get his pulse and his blood pressure up so high that he could not go to sleep even after he had got that fire started again. It was his fault, of course, when the fire went out, for he had never taken the time to learn the whims of this particular heating system, nor had he hired a competent furnace man to take care of the thing for him.

One very bitter night in February he went home late, he and his wife, and as usual he started at once for the cellar, and there he discovered what he. had expected—a cold furnace. He picked up the shovel and started to slam at the fire-box, but then suddenly he decided he was making a terrible fool of himself. He went back up-stairs where his wife awaited him anxiously, for she dreaded these explosions of temper. But there was no explosion this time. He told her very quietly to go on to bed, changed to some old clothes and went back down to the cellar to start a fresh fire. He took a novel with him, and while waiting for the kindling to ignite the coal, he read a few chapters. It wasn't long before he had the fire going, and he himself was ready for sleep.

Next day he told me of the experience.

" I decided I might as well have a little sense," he related. "It's just plain dumb to make bad matters worse."

How obviously correct he was! Nothing is dumber than deliberately to make bad matters worse. Yet that is exactly what I did for a great many years, and exactly what most of us are doing a great part of the time. If business is bad we think gloomily about it, and so make it worse. If we have some little thing wrong with us, we concentrate on it and so make it seem worse, even if we do not make it actually worse.

I like golf, but for many years I failed to discover the real joy of the game. My first regular companion on the links was a man with a furious temper, and when he sliced a shot, or dug a divot, he became temporarily insane. I have seen him break a dub over his knee, and I have seen him wrap several clubs around trees that happened to be handy. My golfing temper was never so vicious as that, but it was bad enough to destroy a great many hours which otherwise might have been happy and whole-some. When I'd made a put and the ball would hang on the rim of the cup, I'd slam the putter on the ground and cuss the ball. Then one day I tried my formula on myself. "Suppose someone ordered you to be such a fool as that," I said to myself, "would you submit?" Of course there was but one answer to the question. I began then to reform my golf manners and habits, and at once my pleasure in the game started to mount. I'm no star now, and never expect to be. Just a good-natured duffer, but there is no man alive who can enjoy a golf game more than I can. Whether I win or lose, make good shots or slice my drives, my enjoyment is the same, for I go out now to play, and not to fight.

Last summer an appeal was sent out by an official of the Boys' Club Fed-eration of America asking golfers not to swear so much before the cad-dies. I am in agreement with that appeal, but I wonder if it would not have been more effective if the well-meaning club official had put the re-verse English on it and sent it out in this form: "Caddies are young boys in the hero-worshiping age. To them you are a man of affairs. They are easily influenced by your views and by your conversation. Will you not, therefore, make as big an ass of yourself as is possible in front of these boys? Swear, tell smutty stories, treat them just exactly the opposite of the way you would like your young son to be treated." The palpable absur-dity and immorality of that plea might have made the point more effectively than a straightway appeal. Anyway, it illustrates the point I am trying to make, which is that we would be a lot better if we were ordered to be worse.

There came into my office one day a man who was down on his luck. He had no money, no job, no anything, according to his story, that was worth having. His case was a tough one, and I gave it a great deal of thought. Obviously, it was not going to be easy to straighten him out, for he seemed to be composed of nothing but kinks. Finally, I suggested to him that he go home and make for me a list of the qualities which he considered necessary for successful living. I told him to take plenty of time, for I wanted him to make the list as complete as possible. He was not at all enthusiastic but agreed to try my plan. I think he agreed only because he felt it nothing more than courteous in return for the time I had devoted to him.

The following week he returned and placed his list on my desk. Meanwhile I had made up a list of the qualities he had exhibited to me. His list showed courage, good humor, love, energy, neatness, clear thinking and health. My list showed gloom, indigestion, bad posture, envy, selfishness and carelessness.

" Here is a list I have written down," I said to him. " Look it over while I am examining yours." I took plenty of time studying the qualities he had set down in order that he might have time to ponder what I had written.

"What's the sense in all this junk you've put down here?" he asked.

"Junk!" I exclaimed. "Fine! That's exactly what it is, and that's what I wanted you to realize."

"Well, I realize it, but what about it?

"Those qualities I have set down have been exhibited by you every time you have come into my office," I told him. "Yet you wonder why you are down on your luck. Here you have given me a list of fine qualities, and you admit that without these no man can succeed. Why, then, do you consistently refuse to reflect a single attribute which you yourself say is necessary for success? Why do you go around reflecting nothing but the opposite of successful qualities? Would you hire a gloomy, stooped, envious dyspeptic? Would you like such a man for an office associate?"

He said he would kick such a fellow out.

"That's exactly what the people to whom you have applied for work have been doing. They've been kicking such a fellow out."

He looked at me in dismay, and I decided to drive my point home.

"Now here is a task for you," I continued. "I want you to throw away this list of fine qualities you have put down, take that list of junk' I gave you, and go forth with it as your guide. Every time you ask for a job, remember to be selfish, careless, envious and gloomy." "You're making fun of me," he objected.

" Not at all," I said. "I'm just telling you to go out of here and continue to be a big fool." "I'll be damned if I do!" declared my caller, now aroused to a higher degree of spirit than I had ever before seen him manifest, which was, I hope, the beginning of an about-face for him.

On a train one day I saw a father and his small daughter traveling together. The father was reading, and the little girl, from loneliness or some other cause, began crying. For a minute or two she cried unheeded by her father, but finally he turned from his newspaper and looked squarely at the child. I thought he was all set to punish her, but he did no such thing.

"Louder!" he ordered. The little girl cried on.

" I told you to cry louder!" said her father, and the child, who seemed a stubborn little trick, stopped crying immediately and began playing with her doll.

That man, too, has discovered that certain persons respond best to what might be called reverse English instructions. Human beings certainly are not standardized. An argument that convinces one will be rejected by another. In my adventures with troubled men and women I try to present my ideas directly or in reverse, depending on the case at hand. The goal is to share my fortune, and the means to that end are of no great importance.

"What business are you in?" a man asked me.

"The expression business," I answered.

"What's that?"

"Trying to express certain qualities in my conduct, and certain ideas in my words."

CHAPTER SEVEN
SALVAGED FORTUNES

ANY experience can be transformed into something of value. I do not say that every experience can be made to show a net profit, spiritually or financially, but that something can be salvaged from it, and very often the salvage will offset any immediate loss incurred by the experience itself. To demonstrate this point I shall relate several stories from life, all of them known to me personally, or through others.

In a community not far from New York City there lives a woman whose life has been one long blessing to many others. She married when very young, and she and her husband started out on a career that gave every promise of happiness.

Hers was a romantic marriage in the highest sense. Childhood sweethearts, then college sweethearts, and finally sweethearts in marriage. He had a good position and was marked out by his employers for rapid and repeated promotions. There was not a cloud in their sky until the blackest of clouds appeared, the cloud of death itself. This perfect union was dissolved by the sudden passing on of the young husband, a death that came before any children had been born.

The young widow faced what seemed complete wreckage. Neither in one year, nor in twenty years, did she ever contemplate remarriage. She is possessed now, as she was at the beginning, by her boy husband. But she was too strong to spend her days in useless grief. She determined to compensate, as far as possible, for the good she was certain her husband would have done had he lived, and after the first few black months, she began to look around to see what she might do. Her income was small, but large enough to take care of her in a meager sort of way.

Robbed of motherhood by the tragic death of her husband, she decided to be a mother to other women's children. She went first to a kinsman whose wife had died, leaving him with several boys and girls. This family she reared to robust and wholesome maturity. Another family then needed her, and she went again to make a second home. This time, too, she was successful. But all of her hours were not required by the duties of this second family, so she began to go from home to home, as necessity arose, waiting upon the sick, taking care of children whose parents wished to get away for brief vacations, substituting for mothers who were ill. Everyone in her whole section knows her, and everyone feels free to call on her. She accepts no money for this service. Many people have tried to pay her. Many of those whom she has succored were able to pay her something, yet she always refused. If they insisted, she would suggest that they make a contribution to her church society. Her actual income is about fifty dollars a month, yet she says it is all she needs. She is old now, but still going the rounds, welcomed everywhere as a deliverer in time of crisis. Her face shows the kind of life she has lived, for it is a happy face. Not merry, but confident and content.

This great life she has lived has not repaid her in full for the loss of her husband. There is no need to be foolish and say that it has, but she has salvaged from a dark adventure a bright career, one that makes all those who know her pause in reverence when they think of her.

A happy-go-lucky, able, handsome young friend of mine was making money in a hurry three years ago. Unmarried, earning a salary much larger than he needed, he was plunging recklessly into the great bull market of 1928.

He bought on margin. He borrowed money and bought more on margin. At the beginning of September 1929, there stood in his name two hundred thousand dollars' worth of stocks, all of them going up. He held to his job, and he worked effectively in it, but none too diligently, for he saw that wealth was to be made much more quickly in the stock-market. Out of his salary he could have saved from three to four thousand dollars a year, but he was impatient. Millions of others were equally as impatient as he.

The crash came, and when it was over my young friend found himself twenty-eight thousand dollars in debt. Not one thing did he save; that is, not one dollar. He had been worth more than forty thousand dollars in actual money, and he was worth, on paper, two hundred thousand, but when the debris of that market collapse was cleared away, he saw himself sunk in a deep and dark hole.

What was he to do? There were two courses open. One was to make bad matters worse by worrying, fretting, drinking, and planning to run out, if possible, on his debts to his broker and his banker. The other was to call up from within his soul the finest elements in his character, face the issue squarely, and work his way out. He decided upon this latter course, and is now paying out as swiftly as he can. He has bought no clothes for two years, but no one would know this unless he told it, for he dresses splendidly on the much too liberal wardrobe he had accumulated in the days of his imagined wealth. He has cut down on his lunches, on his entertaining, on everything. Three hundred dollars each month he devotes to his debts, and on what is left over he lives well enough, though he says he often is pinched for cash.

Before I began the writing of this chapter I went to see him, for the express purpose of asking him some direct questions.

"How much harm did your fall from a fool's paradise do you?" I asked him.

"It did me good," he answered. "Good, I Say, and I mean it."

"How long did it take you to get from under the cloud of gloom that came down on you in the autumn of 1929?" ee l began to see the light after one day," was his answer. "Since then, it has shone brighter for me each day than it did the day before. I am worth much more to my company than I was, for I work harder and more seriously now. I'll win promotion more quickly, and some of these days you may find me an official. That never would have come about if I had cleaned up in the market.

You know me. My temperament was a spending, laughing, fun-loving sort, and a little money would have made me a man ˢ about-town for life. Now I hope to become a pretty fair citizen, one of these days."

That's the outward part of his story. Inwardly, he says, the experience has meant vast riches to him.

"It taught me that material wealth is not necessary. I have now all the things I require. I am as rich as I ever was, except for the money I lost, which I wasn't using, anyway. Did it ever occur to you that if a man had a million dollars in the bank and wasn't using it, he couldn't tell the difference if that million vanished until someone told him it had gone? As long as he thought he had it, he would be rich. I have about concluded that wealth is a state of mind, and that anyone can acquire a wealthy state of mind. Anyway, I'm striving toward that end, and honest, cross my heart, I am glad I went broke, for what I lost in money I have more than gained in character and in seriousness of purpose."

This, I think, is another fair example of good salvage work Some men, poor tragic fellows, killed themselves when they realized their money had gone. Some others became mentally rich through the same experience.

Some years ago I read a story which belongs under the head of salvage, though it has in it no element of tragedy or loss. It is a story of salvage realized from a job that seemed to have no promise. This time I can use the man's name. I am glad to use it, for the story of John A. Spencer has meant much to me. Often I have told it to others.

When he was a youngster Mr. Spencer landed a job as night-watchman in a sawmill, and in addition to his duties as guard he had to keep the fire up. A night-watchman's job certainly isn't very hard, and some of us would find it very difficult to see much hope for advancement from such a start. But Mr. Spencer did a little thinking in the quiet hours of the night, did enough thinking, in fact, to hit on an idea which later became a very valuable invention. He used pine

slabs to keep the fire going, and after throwing some of them into the fire-box he would go outside to sit in the cool. By and by there would be a sharp snap from the fire-box door. Later there would come another similar snap, and this second one was the signal that more slabs should be thrown on to the fire.

Any one might have gone that far with his reasoning, but Mr. Spencer went on from there to some close observation. He noticed that the middle of the round fire door heated more quickly than the rim, therefore expanded, and so caused the first snap. Then, when that center of the iron door cooled again, it would snap back. It buckled out, and buckled back. That is what this night-watchman noticed, and it occurred to him that this fact, the more rapid heating of a metal center than its accompanying metal rim, might be used to advantage. Already he was using it to summon him inside the sawmill, but he had bigger notions in his head.

Finally, he hit on a definite plan for utilizing this fact he had discovered, and there followed year after year of painstaking, patient work with very little reward at first. Eventually, after he had been backed by some other men who had faith in his plan, he emerged with the thermostat invention used in certain electrical equipment to turn off the current when the apparatus becomes overheated. A little metal disk does the work, by heating more quickly in the center than on the rim, snapping in the center and thus cutting off the current. A neat idea, and one that brought a whole lot of good things to the man who put it to work.

Isn't that a good example of a man salvaging something from a situation which seemed to have no wealth hidden in it? To me it is all of that and more.

I wonder how many of his readers know that Clarence Hawkes, lecturer, poet and writer on nature, is totally blind. In his childhood he lost one leg and both eyes. In spite of that he has become a naturalist who is widely respected, a poet who is widely read, an inspiration to thousands of persons. He faced a life of complete darkness. Out of it he salvaged a life of usefulness. For more than forty years he has seen nothing. That is, he has seen nothing except the vast panorama of spiritual truth and beauty. He confessed to a friend of mine that he has his dark moments yet, and always will have them. But the tenor of his life is brilliantly bright, radiantly cheerful. It is the sort of life which makes the rest of us feel ashamed of our own petty fears and inexcusable failures, for here is a man who created greatness out of wreckage.

Scores, hundreds of other blind persons have done the same thing. The possibility of easy accomplishment destroyed; they shove upward through difficulties to high places.

One more story, and I think my point will be sufficiently well illustrated. In this chapter, as you see, I am not sharing my fortune with you, but am writing of others who, by telling their own experiences, have shared their fortunes with me. Surely, there is enough spiritual wealth' in this world, and enough people willing to share their discoveries, to make every one of us a better agent for the great principles of successful living.

Archibald Rutledge is a hunter, and one time he planned a great hunt on an island. The water was high, which made it easy to find game on the island, where both birds and animals had taken refuge on the unflooded ridges. With his Negro hunting companion Mr. Rutledge pad• died over a perilous stretch of water to the island. It was a long hard task to get there, and one they were thankful to have behind them. The small boat was run into some bushes and made fast, then the hunters turned to collect their paraphernalia and go ashore. To their astonishment and dismay they discovered they had forgotten to bring along a gun. A hunt without a gun! What sort of thing would that be? Here was a fine chance to fly into a rage, and to spoil a day, but Mr. Rutledge thought better of it, and decided that instead of hunting with a gun, he would roam the island as a friend to the wild creatures. All day he walked, his delight increasing as the hours passed. He declares that he learned more that day than on any other in his hunting experiences. But he killed nothing at all. The hunt, measured by the contents of the game bag, was a flat failure. But was it a failure? It would have been if the hunter had permitted it to be. Instead, he took his choice between two courses, each obviously open to him. One was to let the failure be a failure, the other was to salvage something from it.

I do not know the full extent of that salvage, but my guess is that in money and in happiness it has amounted to much. One of the best articles Mr. Rutledge ever wrote was about that day's experiences, and that article forms a notable chapter in one of his delightful books. Had all gone as planned on that occasion he would have had some meat for several days. But everything went wrong except his own mental processes, and so he made a lot of money out of the incident. Better still, he gained a new appreciation of wild creatures in times of stress, and he has passed that appreciation on to those of us who read his works.

CHAPTER EIGHT
SPEECH MAKING

WHEN I think of myself, Vash Young, going about the country making addresses to men and women of intelligence and of high standing in business and professional life, I sometimes am tempted to laugh at the absurdity of the thing, and at other times I am shocked at the reality of it. After a speech has been delivered and people come crowding around telling me it helped them, and others write for copies, I almost have to pinch myself in order to be certain it is not an illusion. Certainly the man I was for more than thirty years could have nothing to say that would be listened to, so it must be that this fortune I inherited is the secret. Yes, that is the explanation. When I ceased to be a self-centered person and started out as an instrument for the expression of certain qualities I began to gain attention. Not I, but the qualities. There is nothing unusual about me, nothing important, and nothing profound. I am not even what people know as a story-teller. The applause, therefore, is not for me but for the ideas I express and in which I believe, those same ideas which came to me by inheritance from the demise of my former self, and which I am so eager to share with others.

My start as a speaker was not impressive. At a sales meeting on one occasion I decided to express myself, and I butted right in at the wrong time, and talked at some length about a subject with which I was not familiar. Under such conditions a man generally will keep on talking in the hope that eventually he will say something that shows at least a ray of intelligence. With great determination I blundered on, amid a silence from all others present that should have warned me I was making a fool of myself. Finally I came to the end of my remarks and sat down. Still there was silence. I began to sweat and wonder if I had done as badly as I seemed to have done. At the moment the boss said nothing, but in a day or two I received a letter from him in which this searing sentence appeared: "It is better to remain silent and be considered a fool than to talk and remove all doubt."

That was a straight right to the button and it floored me for a long time. My ambition to become an orator withered, but my determination to learn a little wisdom began to grow. I recalled a story of a young minister who was to be ordained, and who had prepared his first official sermon with great care. To him it seemed a masterpiece. He had practiced it in his room at night. He had gone out into the woods and said it to the trees. Every word, every inflection of the voice, every gesture was carefully studied, and every one seemed to this young man as nearly perfect as could be. He would show his elders what real preaching was!

The hour arrived for him to deliver his great sermon. Down the aisle he came, walking erect and with a sure stride. Up the steps to the pulpit he strode, proud and confident. He faced his audience, lifted his arm in dramatic fashion and in keeping with his rehearsals, but no sound came out of his mouth. That wonderful sermon had taken wings and flown away. He struggled. He reddened. He stammered, drank water and choked, and then, with a drooping head, every muscle in his body limp, he came down those same steps humbly. He took a seat in the rear of the room, his head still hanging, his spirit crushed. An old minister came over to him, tapped him on the shoulder and said.

"My young brother, if you had gone up those steps as you came down, you might have come down as you went up."

That story seemed designed for me, and, added to the letter from my boss, it accomplished complete humiliation. No more false front stuff for me on public occasions. No more bumptiousness. Humility was the thing. Vash Young was nothing, just one of the creeping things which crawl along the earth. But Vash Young, and everyone else, is capable of ex' pressing noble qualities and enduring ideas. Realization of this was my first lesson as a public speaker.

My first important address was at a testimonial luncheon given to me in New York by scores of friends, for most of whom I had written life-insurance policies. I knew long in advance of this luncheon and worked harder than I have ever worked since to prepare an able address. I tried to create some striking phrases. That great speech was never delivered, and it is well for me that it was not. When my time came I spoke spontaneously, and got by with it, for I realized, after listening to the speakers who preceded me, that what I had planned to say, and the manner in which I had planned to say it, would be but a bucket of cold water on an otherwise delightful occasion. Days afterward I read that formal address of mine again, and the thing was unbelievably bad. With a sense of shame that I had prepared it, and gratitude that something had saved me from delivering it, I tore the sophomoric oration up and dropped it silently into my waste-basket. This was my second lesson in speaking. Since then I never have tried to deliver a great talk, nor a formal one. I asked a speaker of wide experience how to proceed henceforth, now that I had learned to be humble and to be spontaneous and natural.

"How do you remember the words of your addresses?" I asked him.

" I never think of the words," he replied. "All I have to remember are the thoughts. Put them down on a piece of paper if you wish, have them clearly worked out in your mind and the wore will come all right."

Upon invitation of business groups I have told of my fortune in New York, Chicago, Pittsburgh, Louisville, Cedar Rapids, Des Moines, Wichita, Denver, Oakland, San Francisco, Los Angeles, Sacramento, Santa Barbara, San Diego, Salt Lake City and many other smaller places. In all of these addresses I told of my fortune to share, and the address seemed to go over well except in Salt Lake City, my home town, where it was a frost. Speakers tell me that is not unusual. A man goes back to his old home high with hope. Through the years he has built up a romantic concept of the old place. He remembers its streets, its people and all the good times he has had there, and in his folly he imagines he has been as much in the minds of the town people as they have been in his. But this rarely is the case. Move away and the old home town forgets you. Why should it not forget you?

You left it, and it has been busy with others who remained and with newcomers. A friend of mine went home after an absence of several years, and, bursting with sentimental eagerness, he started down Main Street. From a distance he saw an old acquaintance approaching, and he almost ran to meet this resident, grabbed his hand and told him how glad he was to see him again.

"Yes, yes," said the resident. haven't seen you in some time. Have you been away?"

It was something like that with me in Salt Lake City. They did not even know I had gone away, nor did many of them know I had come back. Which is as it should be. A city would be a nice mess if its people spent their time remembering and talking about unimportant persons who have drifted off looking for greener pastures.

There are many angles to this speech-making game. One sure-fire thing is for the speaker to tell stories in which he is the goat. Good-natured self-ridicule always gets a laugh. Descriptions of experiences similar to those had by every member of the audience is good stuff, too, for it gives authenticity to a speaker's remarks. But these elements will not of themselves make a speech a success. Most of my talking has been done within the last two years when I could be sure that many persons in front of me were up to their ears in trouble. They needed to laugh, and they needed to recall pleasant adventures of their own, but they needed and wanted something to take home with them and chew on for a while. In all humility I say that my fortune shared with others seems to have done good, for after each address, with but few exceptions, I have received scores of letters, and when the talk has been broadcast by radio, the number has mounted into the hundreds. If my experiences are a true guide, people are hungry for affirmative thinking, for happiness, for ways out of gloom. It is not I they are interested in, nor am I of any use to them, but the ideas I try to express. I can say this because these ideas are not original with me. I am nothing more than a talking-machine with a record on it. In this day of sophistication, actual or imagined, old-fashioned virtues, old-fashioned qualities are often laughed at by the smart boys, but we must live by these same ancient qualities, or disintegration will be our lot. Very frankly I say that never have I thought of anything which was in the slightest original. Any person in the world who will free himself of self-consciousness, think of himself as the agent for the promotion of long-established ideas, can do as well or better than I do as a public speaker. That's a fact.

Seldom have I made a speech without acknowledging my debt to my wife. This is not a sentimental gesture, nor is it a trick, but a sincere and merited giving of credit where it is due. Mrs. Young was brave enough to dance a merry dance with me that night when I went home and told her I was out of a job and had less than a hundred dollars to keep us supplied with necessities. Not a moment did she doubt, and never has she doubted. Most of us, I suspect, are wifemade men. That is why the little tributes I pay to her have been so well received. That, and the fact that in the groups before which I have spoken salesmen have predominated, and every salesman knows that his wife can make him or ruin him. The sales manager for one of the great national enterprises has said -that he regarded the wives of his men as more important than the men themselves. When one of his salesmen is falling down he often visits that man's home and talks with his wife.

Selling isn't easy on the men engaged in it, and it is much less easy on their wives. In many vocations the woman comes first in such matters as the buying of clothes, and if either husband or wife must do without, it is the man who wears the old rags. With salesmen this is not likely to be the case, for a salesman must make a good appearance. When his income is small, his wife must slave at home, in order that he may dress well, eat well and entertain, otherwise he will not rise in his company. He plays golf before she does, for golf is a part of his machinery for making contacts. He remains downtown with the boys, while she remains at home with the children. This is almost standard procedure for young salesmen. They are free spenders, too free. They wear clothes which cost more than their salaries seem to justify. They are the first to come out with straw hats in the spring, and with felt hats in the fall. They must be abreast of the times, or ahead of them. When the family income is small, there is only one way the man can live as a salesman must, or as he thinks he must, and that is for the wife to be a hero at home. The saving element in this situation is that once a salesman starts up, once his income rises to adequate figures, he lavishes money on his wife. He tries to make up to her then for all the hard years she has known, for he, more than any other person in the world, knows how she has saved the pennies in order that he might earn the dollars. When salesmen applaud what I say about my wife, I know that the applause is not for either of us, but for their own wives who that very minute are attending to duties at home.

Frankness I find is one of the finest elements in my address. I never try to disguise what I have to say, nor to coat it with sugar. I am proud to be the medium for the expression of ideas which seem to me essential for the continuity of life. There are as many ways to happiness as there are roads to Rome, and no doubt the people who find nothing in my plan of life, have worked out for themselves plans that are equally as good. I hope this is the case. But be it ever so true, it does not weaken my obligation to share with other average mortals like myself this great fortune of right thinking which came to me when the old Vash Young turned his toes up .to the daisies, and took with him the debris of life which had made him so unhappy and so unsuccessful.

CHAPTER NINE

HERE AND HEREAFTER

AFTER one of my talks a member of the audience said to another: "Oh, he's one of those religious birds." Seemingly, he meant the comment as a criticism, perhaps as an explanation of certain ideas which he thought foolish and utterly unworkable. But whatever was in his mind, I am proud to state that he is right. I am one of those religious birds, and I cannot close any account of my experiences without acknowledging my debt to religion. It is the biggest thing in my life. I believe everything a religious man is supposed to believe, and probably more. Sometimes I hear men almost apologizing for their faith, as though it were some antique thing which no longer is respected by persons of education and intelligence. But in my reading I notice that religion always has been a chief condemn of mankind, and that most men who attain to high places have believed in God. If I must choose between stringing along with men who have done great things, or with those who coitize the things they have done, I prefer the former. Still that is not the reason I am religious, for with me religion is not an imitation of others, nor a blind following in the path of others, but is a scheme of life that works. I cannot say anything about is effectiveness in any life except mine, for I have no way of knowing all the truth about any person except myself. Anyway, it is sufficient for me to know that in my own use the religion I have has proved good for me.

"Do you believe in prayer?" a troubled man asked me.

"Positively!" I replied. "Don't you?"

"I once believed in it, and I still try to, but my experience is that prayers get lost some• where in transit. No answers ever come to mine."

That statement deserved respect, for it came from an honest man. Obviously, I could not tell him with certainty why his prayers had not been answered, but I did have an opinion on the subject

"What do you think about when you are praying?" I asked.

" I think of the mess I am in," was his reply, and perhaps that explains why he found prayer apparently useless to him- His mind was immersed in gloom, and gloom certainly is not an attribute of God. It seems to be fairly plain that if we wish to communicate with God, we should first attempt to be as much like Him as possible. We know that He is not made up of unadmirable qualities. He isn't fear, worry and all that sort of thing. It must be that He is love, courage

and the like. These positive qualities rule the world, and it is difficult for me to understand how a man who goes around reflecting their opposites can hope to get much help from any source. One point upon which everyone will agree is that religion is something to be lived, to be reflected in daily conduct and in motives.

I have had innumerable discussions on religion with people who have come in to see me on "Trouble Day." Some of them have faith in a Supreme Being, some have not, but every one of them, so far as I can recall, would like to have such faith, and many have asked me how to acquire it. The best I can do in a case of this kind is to tell of my own plan. I must remember that "no generalization is due, not even this one." What has been good for me may not be good for another, but since this is a confession of my own experiences, I should like to add a description of what I think religion is.

Religion to me is getting up in the morning and saying gratefully, "Thank you, God, for what I have," instead of, "Please, God, give me a lot more." Gratitude is one of the finest qualities of all. If you think you haven't anything to be grateful for yourself, try to be grateful to God for His goodness to others.

It is trying to make somebody happier for the day before leaving home in the morning. For years I got my wife's breakfast instead of having her get breakfast for me. If this does not appeal to you, try something else that will add to the happiness of some member of your family.

It is pausing long enough in the morning to telephone to some friend or acquaintance who nay need a word of encouragement. In doing this, you develop the habit of thinking of others more than of yourself, and the result will sup prize anyone who gives the plan an honest trial.

It is planning for the day more constructive work than we can possibly. do, and the trying earnestly to do it. Keeping busy is an important part of my religion.

It is the exercise of constant dominion over harmful emotions and false appetites. According to the Bible, God intended man to have dominion over the whole earth. While you may not want to undertake dominion on such a big scale, try having dominion over fear and self, and see what happens.

Religion is the true development of the "giving" habit instead of the " getting" habit. If you don't know what to give, try giving a good wholesome account of yourself each day.

It is eating prudently, playing occasionally, resting sufficiently and keeping in good condition.

It is being tolerant toward the other fellow, no matter what his opinions may be. Religious intolerance is the most regrettable thing I know of.

It is being thrifty in order that upon occasion we may be able to help others and run no risk of becoming a burden to anyone else. The more religion is practiced along this line the better off we will all be.

It is telling other people of the things they have done which merit praise. If we praised as easily as we condemn, what a grand difference it would make in human relationship.

It is common sense applied to all the problems of life. We dream of the things we would like to have instead of doing the things necessary to produce the things we would like to have.

It is the realization that genuine happiness is not only our right but our duty. Anyone can possess it through right thinking and right acting

Finally, religion to me is living now, on this earth, as nearly as possible the life we imagine the next one to be. Are we waiting for a Heavenly state of existence beyond the grave? In my opinion, there is no reason to wait, for we can enjoy Heaven now. Heaven is not a locality, but rather a state of being or consciousness. Let's say we died and went to Heaven. Would it do us any good just to see it? No! The only good we will ever get out of Heaven is to live it in our daily lives—here and hereafter.

Selfishness, pride, greed, envy, malice, dishonesty, jealousy, intolerance, fear, worry, pessimism, depression, hate and anger undoubtedly do not exist in the Heavenly state. If we awake beyond the grave with these things in our consciousness, we will still be living in Hell.

Heaven is unquestionably made up of love, unselfishness, patience, kindness, justice, intelligence, ability, tolerance, charity, peace and joy. Would we be satisfied with such an existence? If so, we can be in Heaven right here on earth, by living these qualities. We will never experience a Heavenly existence, however, except by living these qualities, no matter how many death processes we may go through. As far as I am concerned, this is the "Kingdom of Heaven," and it is within us—now—live it.

Possession of this knowledge is the fortune I wish to share with any who may care to share it with me.

Made in the USA
Las Vegas, NV
29 July 2021